RALPH RAPSON

SKETCHES AND DRAWINGS FROM AROUND THE WORLD

to Bonnie:

With thanks + good travels !

Ralph Rapson

09.18.02

La Parroquia
Great Stone Stairway
Guanajuato, Mexico

Rapson
11·98

RALPH RAPSON

SKETCHES AND DRAWINGS FROM AROUND THE WORLD

foreword by CESAR PELLI

Afton Historical Society Press
Afton, Minnesota

Designed by Mary Susan Oleson
Production assistance by Annie Klas
Edited by Joel Hoekstra

Library of Congress Cataloging-in-Publication Data

Rapson, Ralph, 1914-
    Ralph Rapson: sketches and drawings from around the world / by Ralph Rapson;
    foreword by Cesar Pelli.--1st ed.
        p. cm.
    ISBN 1-890434-49-3
        1. Rapson, Ralph, 1914--Notebooks, sketchbooks, etc. 2. Architectural drawing--United States--20th century I. Title.

NA2707.R364 A4 2001
720'.22'2--dc21   2001041279

Printed and bound in Canada

The Afton Historical Society Press publishes exceptional books on regional subjects.

W. Duncan MacMillan
President

Patricia Condon Johnston
Publisher

Afton Historical Society Press
P.O. Box 100 Afton, MN 55001
1-800-436-8443
aftonpress@aftonpress.com
www.aftonpress.com

FOR MARY

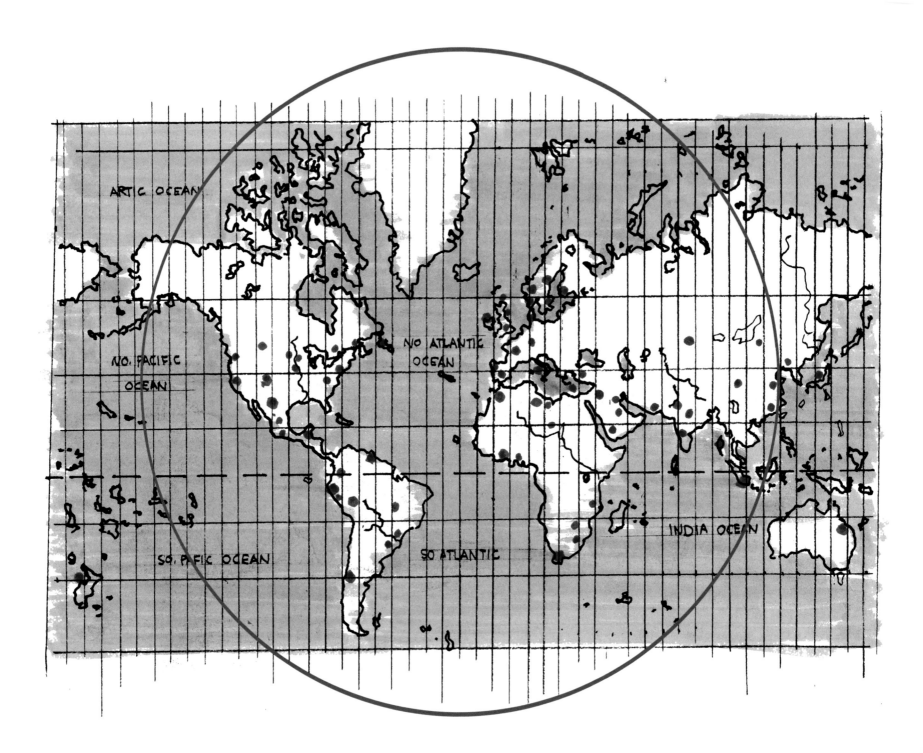

CONTENTS

FOREWORD

WHEN I FIRST CAME TO AMERICA in the 1950s, I found aspects of architecture that were new to me. American architectural drawings at that time were quite different from those I was accustomed to in Argentina or from those that I had seen in European architectural publications. American drawings seemed to be more involved with everyday life, and they seemed to take themselves less seriously than those I knew. I was particularly attracted to the drawings of Ralph Rapson.

Rapson's drawings were fresher, more irreverent, and at the same time more accurate and carried more information than those of any of his contemporaries. Perhaps what was most interesting about his drawings, besides his elegant draftsmanship, was the people in them. They were not just standing there, but they were occupying the architectural space: reading, gardening, cooking, sun-tanning, playing badminton or flying helicopters. The people not only made the drawings more engaging they helped explain how the buildings would be used and enjoyed. They conveyed clear ideas about lifestyle, and this was a new post-war lifestyle: more free, more democratic, and more egalitarian, with an emphasis on leisure-time activities. The people that Rapson drew were obviously enjoying daily life in his buildings.

Rapson's drawings appear at first sight to have been loosely and quickly made, but if we look more carefully we realize that they are accurate and clear depictions of the architecture. For me they had a further attraction: they looked quintessentially American. They were completely self-assured, while at the same time they avoided taking themselves too seriously. This was new and appealing to me.

Perhaps a most important quality of Ralph Rapson's drawings is that the buildings and furniture they described were affordable, designed to be used by people of modest means, that is, by everyone. His designs also seemed to have been done with great pleasure. Rapson embodied, perhaps more completely than anybody else, the ideas of his generation of modern architects in America.

Since those days, I have continued to admire Ralph Rapson and his work: his drawings, his designs for buildings and furniture, and his incredible dedication to architectural education.

CESAR PELLI

I LOVE TO DRAW. I have always enjoyed sketching and drawing for the pure pleasure of it. Also, professionally speaking, drawing is basic to my design process. There is a close and direct relationship between the mind and one's fingers when one begins a design. As one conceives and initiates preliminary design concepts, the ability to document them is essential. To draw intuitively, that is emotionally as well as intellectually, is vital to the process.

Drawing can be a means of researching past experiences and exploring new horizons while developing space and form. It becomes a material aid in the visualization of concepts. Similarly, I enjoy drawing people for the fun of it, but also to convey notions about the use, character, or general ambiance of a place.

In my travels, I have sketched for my own pleasure and also as a way of documenting my experience. Although I carry a camera, I have found that nothing helps me experience and "document" the various aspects of a place or event quite as securely as making a sketch. These sketches and my photographs often serve as starting points for later, more finished, drawings.

In this book, along with these travel drawings, are depictions of a number of notable buildings by fine architects. Additionally, I have included several of my own projects: some as studies, others as more finished drawings. Pencil, ink, crayon, watercolor, felt markers—the media varies, and often consisted of whatever I had at hand.

I have always searched out the old, the unusual, and the new in my travels. Historic or commonplace, beautiful or mundane, people or places—everything is potential subject matter.

RALPH RAPSON

INTRODUCTION

Military Academy Synagogue Niger Desert Israel 1961
Zui Hecker Architect

ONE OF THE BENEFITS of teaching is that it has given me many contacts around the world. I lectured in South Africa at the invitation of colleagues there and have spent much time in Egypt touring with students. But my tour of north-western Africa—Morocco, Nigeria, and Algeria—was doubly pleasurable in that I was able to visit a professional counterpart who was also a former student.

I traveled to Lagos in the early 1970s to help University of Minnesota Professor John S. Myers set up a school of environmental design at the University of Nigeria. One day we made the trip to neighboring DAHOMEY, one of the smallest and most highly populated republics in western Africa. (It is interesting to note that Dahomey was the base for the fabled Amazon women warriors, who terrorized all those with whom they came into contact.) There we visited a village of several hundred homes and other structures built on stilts. It was an amazing sight—this town of thatched roofs and ingenious wood carvings. The people made their way from building to building in long elegant boats carved from solid tree trunks.

Sun-baked CASABLANCA, where I stopped a few weeks later, is comparatively a modern city but equally intriguing. The awnings, robes, people, food—everything was colorful. As I made my way through the markets and streets, however, I was cautious. Amid the narrow maze of passageways, it would have been easy to get lost—though I was usually accompanied by two or three little kids trying to sell me things.

AFRICA

Market Square
Casablanca Morroco

Lake Dwellings on Ganvie inlet
Dahomey Africa

13

SOUTH AFRICA

IN 1983, I SPENT TEN WEEKS lecturing in South Africa at the invitation of a group of local architects and architectural schools. One of my hosts was an architect who had worked for me in Stockholm in the early 1950s while I was designing American embassies.

The landscape of South Africa is rich and varied, filled with mountains, deserts, vineyards, and plantations, and there is some fine architecture, in both the vernacular and contemporary sense. I made many drawings and paintings of Dutch Colonial buildings, with their heavy scrolls and stepped gables.

A day trip took me to JAN VAN WIJK'S AFRIKAANS TAAL MONUMENT near Milnerton. Coming upon this dynamic structure, I imagined for a second that I had suddenly been transported to the moon. The hammered reinforced-concrete form reflects the origin and growth of the Afrikaans tongue.

bone white relief patterns

red tile roof

brown wood frames white windows

deep green leaves pink & cream flowers

colored glass

carved wood doors

pattern in walls

red-terra cotta colored tiles

white paint

BP Center, Cape Town, South Africa
Revel Fox Architect

Wijk's Afrikaans Taal Monument near Milnerton

Small church near Capetown

15

MARY AND I VISITED Brazil just once. It was during the mid-1980s, when my work as a member of the State Department's architectural advisory committee required occasional visits overseas to assess the facility needs of American embassies. While we were there, we traveled to BRASÍLIA, the seat of government designed by Lucio Costa in the late 1950s.

Brasília serves as the hub of a new transportation and communications network that has opened up the vast Brazilian hinterland. I was also taken with RIO DE JANEIRO, the nation's cultural capital and a jewel of a city. Its twisting streets, turquoise shoreline, and beautiful men and women were dazzling. A tram to the top of the fabled Sugarloaf Mountain afforded us a bird's-eye view of the city and the white sweep of Copacabana Beach.

As is my custom, I also wandered a bit. On this particular trip I spent some time sketching the ornate facade of a SPANISH COLONIAL CHURCH that caught my eye.

Rio de Janeiro Brazil
Sugarloaf Mountain is nestled between the mountains and the sea

BRAZIL

Brasília new capital of Brazil 1960

The Palace of the National Congress Brasillia 1960
Oscar Neimeyer Architect

Parish Church of Pilar Brazil   Salvador Baia 18th Century

New Brunswick small coastal village

CANADA

THE CANADIAN NATIONAL RAILROAD spans the whole of Canada from east to west. My wife and I once traveled the route, stopping at many of the hotels and scenic parks the railroad promoted in its early years as a way of attracting passengers. Among the more memorable stops was the splendid CANADIAN NATIONAL HOTEL in Québec City. The wild expanses of British Columbia were equally intriguing. At the end of the line, I became acquainted with the NATIVE ART OF THE PACIFIC NORTHWEST. I also had a chance to visit the magnificent modern city of Vancouver before embarking on a ship for the English outpost of Victoria.

This was the first of numerous trips I would make to Canada, many of them as a consultant for the University of Manitoba at Winnipeg. I also made a point of visiting SCARBOROUGH COLLEGE, part of the University of Toronto in Ontario. This megastructure housed an entire college campus—including dormitories, offices, and classrooms—under one roof. At the time, it was an innovative approach, and it remains a notable architectural achievement.

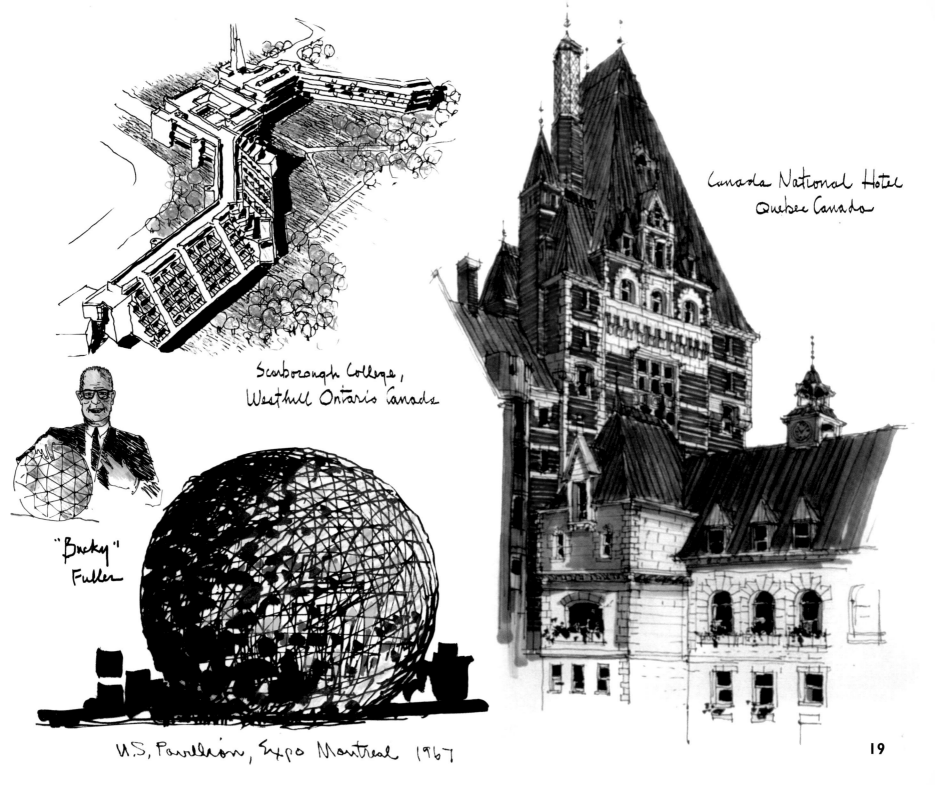

Scarborough College,
Westhill Ontario Canada

Canada National Hotel
Quebec Canada

"Bucky"
Fuller

U.S. Pavillion, Expo Montreal 1967

19

Typical traditional Court house

CHINA

MY PLANS CHANGED, but originally I had intended to go to China right after college. I was struck by the country's unfathomable mystery, vast history, and reputation for inventiveness. In my studies, for example, I had read about UNDERGROUND SHELTERS that Chinese peasants would carve into the sides of mountains or hillsides. On one of my many visits, I was brought face to face with one of these shelters. Some Chinese still live in them, papering the

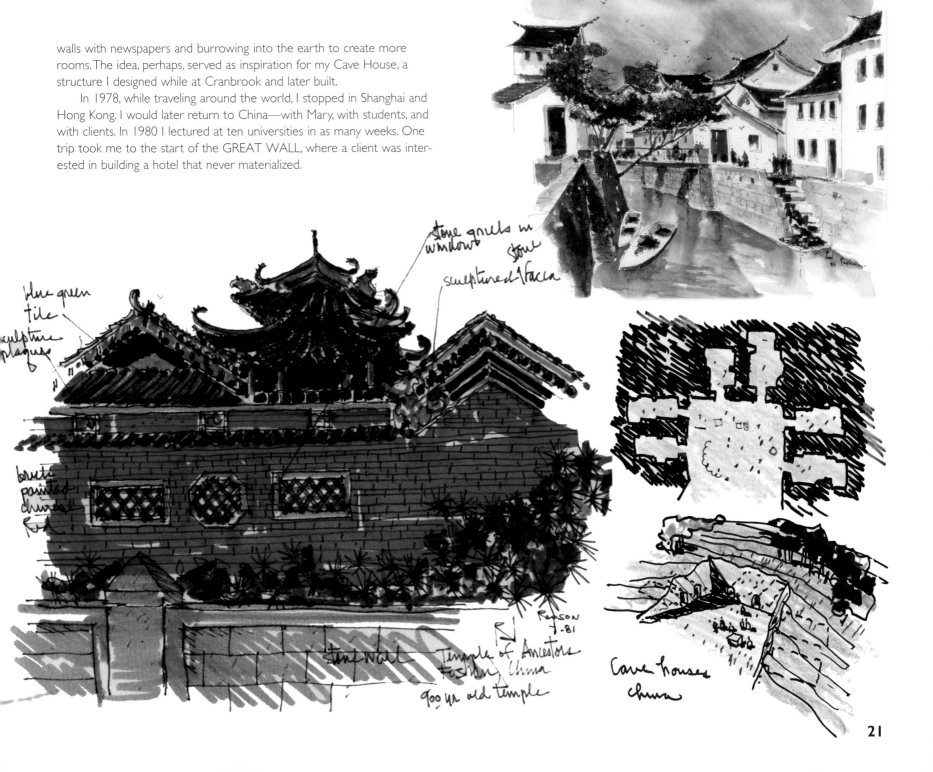

walls with newspapers and burrowing into the earth to create more rooms. The idea, perhaps, served as inspiration for my Cave House, a structure I designed while at Cranbrook and later built.

In 1978, while traveling around the world, I stopped in Shanghai and Hong Kong. I would later return to China—with Mary, with students, and with clients. In 1980 I lectured at ten universities in as many weeks. One trip took me to the start of the GREAT WALL, where a client was interested in building a hotel that never materialized.

blue green tile sculpture plaques

brick painted chinese Red

stone grills in windows stone sculptured facea

Stone Wall

Temple of Ancestors Foshan, China

900 yr old temple

Cave houses China

Ralson 7-81

FROM *THE LITTLE MERMAID* in the harbor and Tivoli
Gardens to its beautiful parks, streets, and fine buildings, both
old and new, Copenhagen ranks as one of the great cities of
the world. My longtime friend Catherine Bauer Wurster, the
foremost early city planner, once wrote that Copenhagen is
one of the world's most beautiful cities.

Interesting and delightful fishing villages dot the shore-
lines of lakes and water inlets throughout Denmark. Shown
here is a TYPICAL VILLAGE, with its jumble of steep clus-
tered roofs in red, orange, and sepia-colored tiles.

DENMARK

U.S.
EMBASSY
COPENHAGEN, DENMARK
RAPSON VANDER MEULEN
ARCHITECTS
20 JAN 52

HOLLAND IS SUCH AN AGREEABLE and beautiful country—every inch of land is loved and sympathetically cared for. Its acres and acres of colorful tulips are unmatched elsewhere and can never be forgotten.

The Hague, where we designed a new U.S. embassy, is a spacious seat of government, diplomats, fine mansions, impressive building facades, and green parks—over fifty percent of the land is devoted to gardens and parks. The city museum also boasts one of the most impressive collections of Van Gogh's work.

Copenhagen's Little Mermaid

'Red wood shoes go mod'

HOLLAND

intense blue sky
cream sandstone
strong shadows

col. head
papyrus flower

stone cols.
decorated with
stylized carvings
low + sunken relief

stone face
somewhat
grayed gum color

no mortar in
stone joints

The Temple of Amun at Karnak,
Thebes Egypt (290 B.C.)

EGYPT

I HAVE TRAVELED TO EGYPT a number of times, once with a group of University of Minnesota architecture students on a side excursion from our semester of study in Europe, and again when our firm won an international competition to design the headquarters for the Egyptian National Petroleum Products Institute in Cairo.

But I was alone for the few days I spent in Luxor, the city of temples. My hotel was a stone's throw from the TEMPLE OF AMUN-RE at Karnak, one of the most important. Because of the heat, I had the place almost entirely to myself. I made several visits to

Typical street scene in old Cairo

Mohamed Ali Mosque

Amun-Re, and was fascinated by the massive size of the weathered columns, the magnificent hieroglyphic carvings that tell ancient stories, and the play of sun and shadow in the complex. I have long been drawn to Egyptian civilization and have read several novels and histories on the subject, but like most architects, I am most puzzled by the construction: How did these ancient peoples erect obelisks, giant temples, and the pyramids? It remains one of the world's great architectural mysteries.

The visitor to CAIRO, on the other hand, is never alone. The city's streets are crowded, dusty, and noisy. But even here, I couldn't help but imagine myself as a figure in history, the shadows of the ancients sliding along the narrow streets next to me.

LONDON IS ONE OF THE WORLD'S finest metropolitan centers, representing an immense reservoir of history and culture. Even after several visits I found it difficult to assess the great richness of the city. The lofty clock tower BIG BEN and the architectural quality of the adjacent PARLIAMENT buildings form perhaps the most famous symbol of London.

Touring with Mary at the wheel

Mysterious, prehistoric Stonehenge

ENGLAND

The Guards at Buckingham Palace

The Houses of Parliament and Big-Ben alongside the River Thames

A weekend trip to see plays and do some shopping first took Mary and me from Amsterdam to London in the early 1950s. We made several similar visits to the city thereafter, always impressed with the museums, pubs, and the proper way the English queue up for everything rather than pushing and jostling their way to the front of the line.

But it was the countryside that I found most charming, with its wandering stone walls and bucolic byways. We made several excursions along the coasts, a trip to Stonehenge, and other forays out and about.

State Governmental Palace; Quito, Equador, 1941
Ralph Rapson Architect

ECUADOR

I WAS MORE THAN EAGER to travel to Quito, once the center of an advanced Indian civilization and Ecuador's current capital. Some years previously, with my friend, architect Robert Bruce Tague, I had won an international competition for a new legislative complex in Quito. Unfortunately, for reasons never made clear to me, the project was not commissioned. I very much wanted to see what was built instead.

The opportunity came on a trip through western South America in the mid-1970s. The legislative building—which resembled my design not a whit—functioned poorly. But the city, which lies near the equator was interesting nonetheless. A beautiful thirty-minute drive across the highlands and through several small villages brought Mary and me to a small crude monument marking the LINEA EQUINOCCIAL, as determined by an eighteenth-century French survey in the area.

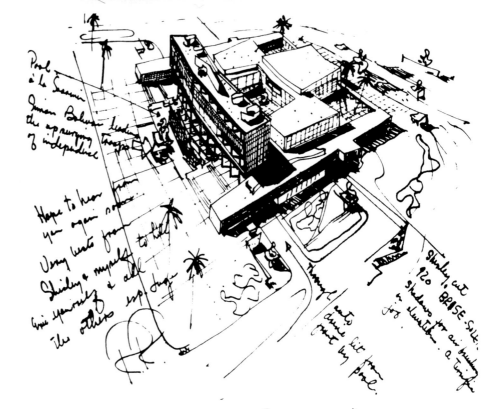

Preliminary study

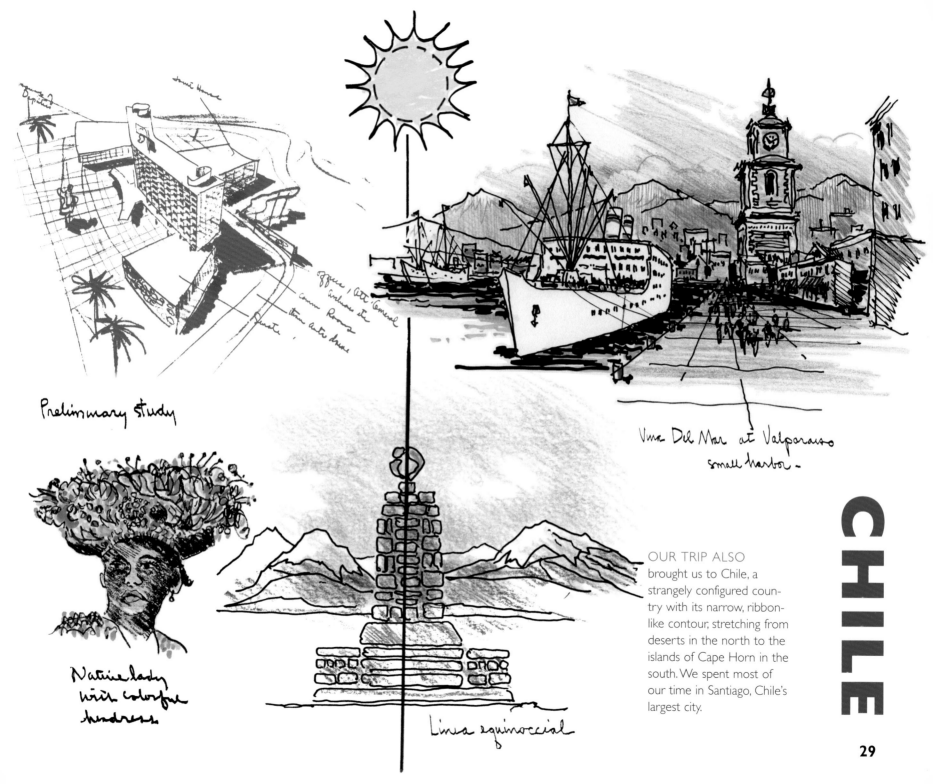

Preliminary study

Viña Del Mar at Valparaiso
small harbor –

Native lady
with colorful
headdress

Linia equinoccial

OUR TRIP ALSO
brought us to Chile, a
strangely configured country with its narrow, ribbon-
like contour, stretching from
deserts in the north to the
islands of Cape Horn in the
south. We spent most of
our time in Santiago, Chile's
largest city.

CHILE

THE ARTS, INCLUDING ARCHITECTURE, have always played a basic role in Finland's cultural history. The harsh Nordic climate demands special awareness of materials, energy, and light. Nature is central and buildings are placed into the landscape with great care.

Unfortunately, my time in Finland, with its lush virgin countryside, endless lakes, and magical green forests, was somewhat limited. Even so, I was able to witness people's love and respect for their land and their love of beauty and quality—in both nature and human-crafted design. Helsinki, the nation's capital and largest city, is wonderfully modern. Everywhere, the architecture is uncluttered and functional, pure, and often beautifully understated.

Father-and-son architects Eliel and Eero Saarinen, of course, had roots in Finland. While at MIT, I also had the good fortune to teach with another son of Finland, Alvar Aalto. Aalto had been invited to design Baker Hall, a new student dormitory. Normal methods were not Aalto's way of teaching: rather, he rounded up any and all willing students and herded them off to a coffeehouse or bar for a cup of joe or round of vodka. He could go on for hours, spinning stories—every one of them meaningful.

Aalto's bentwood furniture also inspired me. He was, along with the Thonet Company, the first to utilize modern technology to produce laminated furniture.

Recent generations of architects continue the long tradition of contemporary design. This is particularly true of religious and secular centers, such as the MYYRMAKI CHURCH-PARISH CENTER in Helsinki.

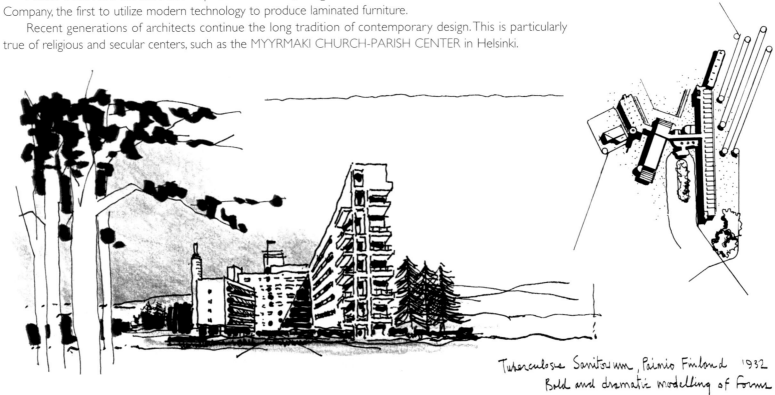

Wood Technology Laboratories I.T. Otaniemi Finland 1964 Alvar Aalto

Tuberculosis Sanitorium, Paimio Finland 1932 Bold and dramatic modelling of forms

FINLAND

Hvittrask Kvkkonumme Finland 1902
Arhitects home and studio

Finish Church/parish center at Myyroonaki Helsinki
John Leiviska Arh

Cathedral Helsinki
with Statue of Alexander II of Russia

31

"Waiting for a Tourist"

Typical Street Intersection

FRANCE

ANOTHER STOP—OUR LAST—on my three and a half years of designing embassies and buildings for the U.S. State Department was France. Shortly after our son Rip was born, Mary and I left Germany for Paris. We were designing projects in Athens, Stockholm, and half a dozen other European cities, and the City of Lights served as a convenient base—a short flight away from almost anywhere in Europe. We would stay there two years—the longest we would live anywhere during our time on the continent.

Our first apartment was on the top floor of a building on Ile Saint-Louis. The view was beautiful. We could see out over the island, and NOTRE DAME rose in the distance. With its balanced

Notre Dame Cathedral, Paris

proportions, patterned solids and voids, and harmonious combination of horizontal and vertical elements, the cathedral is perfection itself. I made many drawings of the church, which I greatly preferred to the city's other beloved sacred site, SACRÉ COEUR.

In fact, we saw and experienced much of Paris, familiar and not. We spent a winter clad in sweaters and boots after renting a drafty artist's studio in Montmartre, the bohemian neighborhood immortalized by Toulouse-Lautrec. We spent our last few months in an elegant traditional apartment in Parc Monceau. Even after we returned to America at the request of MIT officials, who wanted me to return to my teaching duties, Paris remained in our hearts—a city both Mary and I loved.

Sacre-Coeur Basilica, Paris

33

GERMANY

Sketch of a typical small German Village Square

100 year old castle, German near Broken in the Münsterland

Along the Rhine Valley Germany

FOR SIX MONTHS WE LIVED in Germany, where I designed a proposal for the American consulate at Bremen and several other structures, and where, incidentally, my son Rip was born in Venusberg, a suburb of Bonn. VIP receptions and afternoon outings took us to cities and villages throughout the German countryside, and I always marveled at the German approach to urban development.

These drawings of MEERSBURG and COLOGNE, for example, depict the charm and elegance common to many old German towns, but in and around these city centers are rings of modern developments and housing. In contrast to American tendencies toward unchecked sprawl, when growth is necessary, it is planned and carried out in a controlled and orderly manner. German cities are compact and do not extend endlessly into the surrounding landscape, which is valued and preserved. The line between city and country is often sharply drawn.

Severin Bridge Cologne, 1960 Dycherdff & Widmann.

Meersberg on the steep shores of Lake Constance, Germany
a small town famous for its wines.

EVEN A MODERNIST must pay homage to the accomplishments of Greece, a country rich in history, theater, literature, sculpture, art, and, of course, architecture. I traveled many times to the ancient country while working on the American embassy in Athens, and first visited the ACROPOLIS with Mary one night under a full moon. That visit was most memorable: the lunar light and shadows seemed to fill the gaps eroded away by the ages.

Old Athens and the villages of the Greek Islands never failed to charm me. Set against azure skies and seas, the boxlike configurations of MYKONOS and SANTORINI seem to tumble down the hillsides of the coast. The houses have been whitewashed so many times that their edges have softened.

Mykonos, Aegean Islands

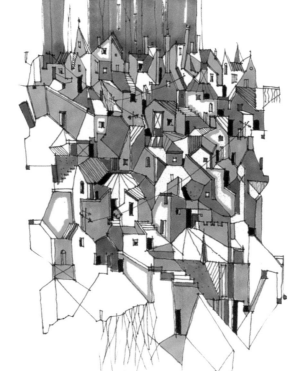

Abstract sketch of a typical Greek Island village

Northern slope of the Acropolis lies Plaka - the old and popular quarter of Athens

Santorini

R. Rep Con
1·16·98

Santorini Greek Islands Aegean Sea

37

ONE OF MY TRIPS AROUND GREECE brought me to the town of NAUPLIA, also known as Nauplion, on the Peloponnesus. At moments the castle high up the mountain seemed like a sandcastle built on the edge of the sea.

Another excursion took me to the Isle of Corfu. Once the site of many ancient wars the island was extremely peaceful. The luxurious groves of oranges, lemons, cork and olive trees here as throughout Greece are simply beautiful.

GREECE

Small church on Corfu Island in the Ionian Sea.

Nauplia, Bay of Nauplia, Greece
with great stronghold on vast rock
of Palamidi in background.

Chios, Aegean Sea

Ralph Rampton
2.10.90

39

Fathpur Sikri

INDIA

ON MY FIRST TRIP TO INDIA, I had been advised to see the TAJ MAHAL by full moon, if possible. Built in Agra by Shah Jahan as a mausoleum for his beloved wife, the white marble structure stands amid dozens of acres of landscaped promenades and reflecting pools.

The crowds of tourists had vanished by the time I reached the Taj, and I was virtually alone as I walked the grounds, which were bathed in milky moonlight. It was a profound experience, equaled in my life only by similar viewings of the Acropolis and Machu Picchu.

My sojourn occurred in 1975, while I was making my way around the world. I visited Bombay, New Delhi, Chandigarh, and a handful of other cities where former students or associates lived. But I was most eager to see FATEHPUR SIKRI, a now-vacant city begun in 1571 and mysteriously abandoned fifteen years later. As I wandered about, I marveled at the

sensitive detail of its design, its character, and its grandeur, and I was fascinated by the life-sized chessboard in the courtyard. Legend has it that real people served as the game pieces, deployed by the orders of a real prince. I was eating my lunch and pondering this unusual complex when suddenly I realized that my sandwich and myself were covered with thousands of red ants. Swatting at the insects, I practically had to strip off my clothes to rid myself of the pests. Little boys surrounded me, laughing as I danced about. It was a memorable ordeal.

Dark Red stone
bright cream stone

Parliament House New Delhi

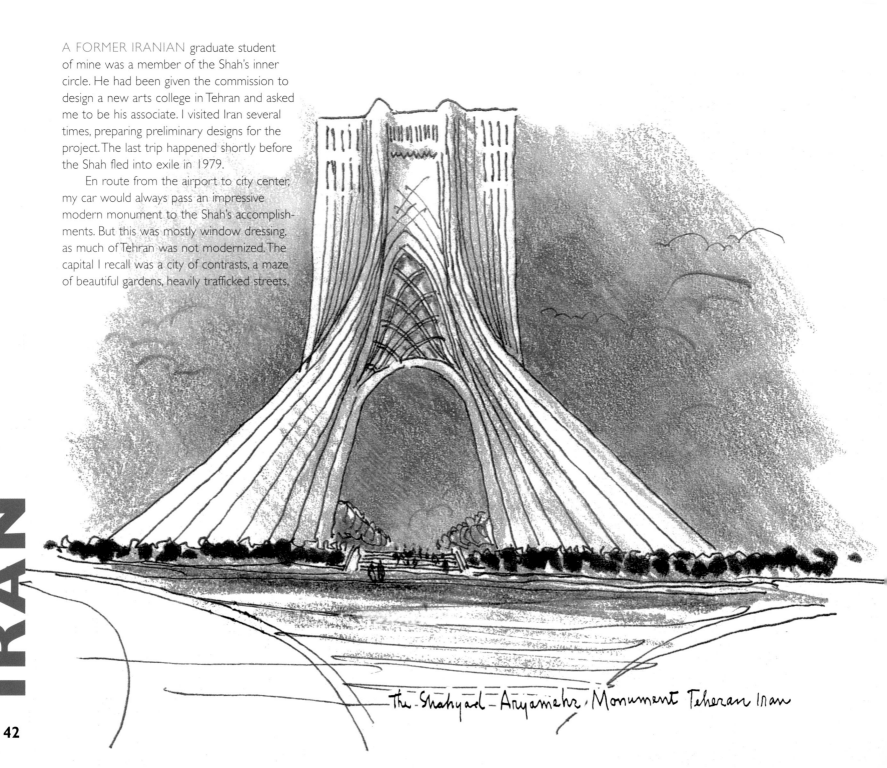

A FORMER IRANIAN graduate student of mine was a member of the Shah's inner circle. He had been given the commission to design a new arts college in Tehran and asked me to be his associate. I visited Iran several times, preparing preliminary designs for the project. The last trip happened shortly before the Shah fled into exile in 1979.

En route from the airport to city center, my car would always pass an impressive modern monument to the Shah's accomplishments. But this was mostly window dressing, as much of Tehran was not modernized. The capital I recall was a city of contrasts, a maze of beautiful gardens, heavily trafficked streets,

IRAN

The Shahyad-Aryamehr Monument Teheran Iran

42

Two traditional small villages in Iran
with "wind-scoops" to catch and circulate air to lower
basements then up – a form of airconditioning.

low-quality housing, and covered bazaars loaded with fascinating goods: jewelry, rugs, fabrics.

I was invited to give a lecture at an international gath-
ering of architects sponsored by the Shah and his wife, a
patron of the arts. I spent a glamorous, fascinating evening at
a party at one of the Shah's homes—a fabulous place constructed of a series of domes, one of which opened, allow-
ing the stars to reflect in the interior pools below.

The Iranian people were friendly, and I often wandered
around small villages to watch the craftsmen working.
Although we did not speak the same language, we could
always communicate.

ITALY FOLLOWED GREECE on a ten-week University of Minnesota study tour I led in 1976. I was as delighted as my students to see Florence, Milan, Rome, and Venice. In the city of canals, we spent countless hours in the PIAZZA SAN MARCO, a spot I always refer to as "the world's greatest outdoor living room."

I spent several days searching out Palladio's work in and around Vicenza, not far from Venice. Here he built some of his finest villas as country retreats for wealthy landowners. One of the best is VILLA ROTONDA. Classical in its purity, balance, and symmetry, the structure stands in composed contrast to the riot of colorful landscape that surrounds it.

Without question, Venice is one of the most remarkable cities. Everywhere one is reminded of the unique marriage of land, water, and buildings—and the fragile nature of the place.

In Florence, of course, we visited the BRUNELLESCHI'S DUOMO, a truly handsome building. Looking back, I'm particularly pleased with my rendering of the church. Carefully done and accurate in proportion as I could make it, the drawing seems to capture the sculpture and the detail of the spiritual shrine.

Villa Rotonda, Vicenza Italy
One of Palladio's best projects

ITALY

Piazza San Marco, Venice Italy 1500s

44

Santa Maria della Salute, Venice Italy
with magnificent Titians and Tintorettos is located directly
across the mouth of the Grand Canal

Venice, Italy

S. Maria del Fiore, Cathedral, Florence, Italy

45

She Wolf. Mother of Romulus and Remus

Baths of Caralla, Rome
powerful structural reminder of "Rome Eternal"

ROME, ITALY

I WAS FORTUNATE TO BE able to spend a fair amount of time in Rome both as a tourist and a working architect. Full of history, energy, and architecture—it still seems the center of a far-flung empire.

There's much to see in Rome and the surrounding countryside, but I was continually drawn to the SPANISH STEPS. What an enchanting place! More than just a unique mix of building types, uses, materials, and colors, the steps are a meeting place for people both night and day. The pace—with all the coming and going, the sitting and standing, the symphony of song and voice, musical instruments, laughter, children calling and crying—always left me energized. Whether with students or fellow architects or alone, I loitered there whenever possible.

St. Peters Basilica, Vatican City, Rome.
The largest church in the world: completed 1626

Farm complex in center of the Trulli district near Alberobello in the heal of Italy

Spanish Steps Rome

the great sweep of the baroque steps connects the Piazza di Spagna with the Pincio Hill and Church of Trinita del Monte

Castle Sant 'Angelo, Rome
Colossal and grim, erected as a mausoleum for Emperor Hadrian

THE JAPANESE HAVE MANAGED to integrate their new and old buildings better than most other nations. Ancient temples and modern apartment towers coexist contentedly in the same neighborhoods. Local architects understand their culture and traditions, even if they prefer contemporary designs.

Traditional timber constructions are characterized by clear, minimal, often austere architectural expression and often coupled with such delicate, poetic elements as paper screens. In contrast, many modern designs—like Kiyonori Kikutake's proposal to expand Tokyo's living space with wart-speckled, tall apartment buildings—are complex, bold, and heavy. Although the towers are highly unique, there is a kind of inexplicable continuity with traditional Japanese design. My several visits to Japan have been extremely rewarding in aiding my understanding of the relationship of traditional and modern architecture and what it says about a people and their culture.

JAPAN

Daibutsuden NARA

Wood Temple in Kyoto   Largest all wood structure in Japan

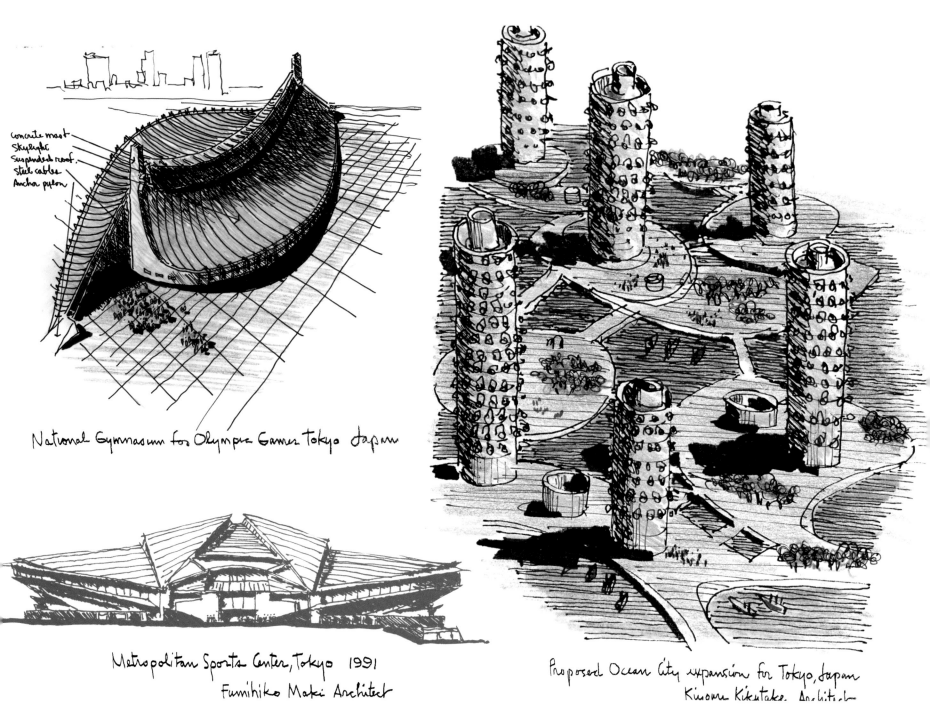

concrete mast
Skylight
Suspended roof
steel cables
Anchor pylon

National Gymnasium for Olympic Games Tokyo Japan

Metropolitan Sports Center, Tokyo 1991
Fumihiko Maki Architect

Proposed Ocean City expansion for Tokyo, Japan
Kiouru Kikutake Architect

49

MARY, OUR TWO YOUNG BOYS, RIP AND TOBY, AND I had no particular plans as we wandered through Mexico for four months in the mid-1950s. We took the train or bus wherever we wanted to go—often small towns or historic sites well off the beaten path. We saw CHICHÉN-ITZÁ, Mitla, and Uxmal—solid testimony to the sophistication and advancement of ancient Mayan civilization—but also spent a memorable week at a remote hacienda where the feasting never stopped and the swimming pool was fed by an old mountain aqueduct.

Today travelers rarely have a chance to rub shoulders with real locals, but we often found ourselves trading smiles and broken English with the native folk as we saw the Mexican landscape—towering mountains, massive plateaus, and unexplored jungles, all under perpetually sunny skies. Despite our distance from home, Rip and Toby were rarely without playmates. They had brought along baseball bats, and we weren't long anywhere before a circle of local youth had gathered wanting to play "bees-ball."

Aztec warr or stone rubbing

MEXICO

Latin American Tower
Mexico City Mexico

Pyramids at Teotihuacán in archeological zone of
San Juan Teotihuacán

Abstract sketch of Island Janitzio

Village of Janitzio Lake Patzcuaro
with giant statue of the patriot Father Morelos

CHICHEN-ITZA
Temple of the Warriors

El Castillo, the four sided pyramid at Chichen Itza

Santa Prisca Church Taxco de Alarcón Mexico
Exquisite example of the Churriguersque style.

FEW MEMORIES CAN COMPARE with my recollections of MACHU PICCHU. Stopping in Peru on our way to Ecuador and Chile, Mary and I boarded a small train from Cuzco with just two passenger cars headed to the ancient mountain city. Few of the passengers were tourists. We followed a stream up into the mountains, took a bus up a zigzagging road, and eventually arrived at a small rundown hotel, where we checked in. Only a handful of people remained as the afternoon wore on and the sun began to set, and we not only wandered among the Inca ruins by moonlight, but also rose early the next morning to watch the sun burn the cloud cover off this ancient aerie.

A few nights later we found ourselves headed by train to Arequipa, the White City. The passage through the Andes Mountains was bitterly cold, and Mary and I were without the heavy woolen sweaters that the locals wore. Shivering and sleepless, we finally arrived at the southern city—a gleaming complex dominated by white volcanic stone constructions and surrounded by eucalyptus and lush fields. I was particularly taken with SANTA CATALINA, once a walled convent where nuns were kept in complete solitude and outsiders were not allowed. All services, food, and supplies were brought in by being hoisted up and over the walls.

PERU

Machu Picchu Peru
mysterious "Lost City" with towering granite peak Huayna Pic
"Temple of the Moon" to the NE behind,

Santa Catalina nunnery Arequipa
the "White City" Peru.

53

General overview of the city of Lisbon, Portugal

PORTUGAL IS ONE OF MY favorite countries. Its coast, mountains, and hill towns are similar to those in the Greek Islands. Flowers and plantings are everywhere. And tourists seem not to have overrun this gem.

Two international architectural juries brought me to Lisbon for a few weeks in the late 1970s. One was for a project on Madeira Island, the other for a new town in southern Portugal. The port of Lisbon makes quite a wonderful city, featuring a beautiful library, busy plazas, and open-air markets that are connected via narrow, tight, and twisting streets. The LISBON CATHEDRAL was built both as a place of worship and as a last bastion of defense in case of war. The proof is in the two towers, flanking the facades, and its battlements.

the Cathedral of Lisbon 1147

54

Dona Maria Pia Bridge Oporto, Portugal 1877

a dramatic and delicate steel structure designed
by Gustav Eiffel, engineer, who designed the Eiffel Tower, Paris

OBIDOS PORTUGAL

55

MY ARCHITECTURAL HISTORY courses at Michigan barely acknowledged the contributions of nations outside Europe and America. Nonetheless, I eventually happened upon some images of architecture from other continents. Among the ones that most fascinated me were several from Russia and Tibet.

A trip to Moscow in 1998 allowed me to view a country where Marxist theories have long since crumbled as a potent political force. I was familiar with certain elements of the city's architecture, due in large part to televised news clips of Soviet military parading across Red Square. But the onion domes of ST. BASIL'S—the backdrop for many of those marches—were more imposing up close. Studying the building's profile and wandering the labyrinthine interior, I came to appreciate the pile of unique and seemingly conflicting forms that make up the structure's style. If nothing else, the Russian Orthodox architecture stands in sharp contrast to the dull, heavy, Communist-era buildings that populate much of the rest of the city.

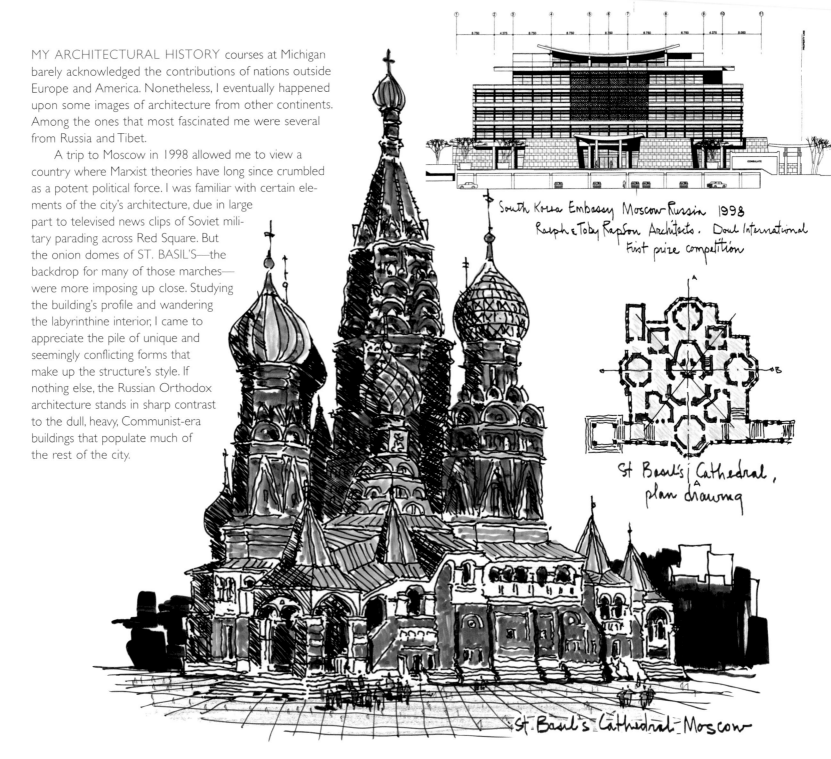

South Korea Embassy Moscow Russia 1998
Ralph & Toby Rapson Architects. Doul International First prize competition

St Basil's Cathedral, plan drawing

St. Basil's Cathedral, Moscow

RUSSIA

COMMUNISM IS STILL THE RULE in Tibet. While visiting China for a conference in 1984, I was lucky enough to land a seat on a plane to the remote kingdom of Lhasa, now a part of China, where travel by foreigners is severely restricted. Traveling with my translator, I arrived in the late afternoon and hurried to see the fortress-like POTALA PALACE. A former monastery, the palace towers over tiny Lhasa and is flanked by an impressive backdrop, the sky-scraping Himalayas. The entire scene glowed golden in the sun and, although I was back on the plane to the conference the next morning, the experience remains deeply embedded in my memory.

Men and horses - a way of life

The Potala Palace
Palace of the Dalai Lama
Lhasa Tibet

TIBET

THOUGH THE HIGHLANDS OF SCOTLAND do not rank among the world's highest mountains, the area is renowned for its historic lore, rugged beauty, and ancestral castles. With Mary driving on the "wrong side of the road," we toured the coast of Fife, lodged in Edinburgh and visited EILEAN DONAN castle on Loch Duich—perched on a rocky spur high above the icy lake and once the scene of famous sieges and bloody raids.

Eilean Donan Castle on Loch Duich Scotland

SCOTLAND

CROSSING OVER TO IRELAND, we continued to travel without an itinerary. But I did have one stop in mind: the GIANT'S CAUSEWAY, near Bushmills. The 37,000 basalt columns, mostly perfect hexagonals formed by the cooling of molten lava, that comprise this formation are truly astonishing. Legend has it that a mythic warrior laid the causeway to reach his ladylove across the sea on a Scottish isle where similar features are found.

Dr. Samuel Johnson, when asked by his biographer James Boswell whether this wonder of the world was worth seeing, replied, "Worth seeing? Yes, but not worth going to see." That was shrewd judgment in 1770 when roads were primitive enough to turn a journey into an expedition.

St Monance Fife Scotland
typical small fishing village.

the Giant Causeway

IRELAND

59

SINGAPORE, LOCATED AT THE VERY southern tip of Malaysia on the straight of Malacca, is a bustling and modern city. It is both one of the busiest harbors in the world, as well as being an independent city state. Fabled for its often mysterious past, it is a complex mixture of old customs and present day commerce.

The temple of Brahamesura, although located in India, is very close to the eastern boundary of the country and is similar to much of the architecture of that region. The structure is composed of two large connected forms, one being an assembly hall and the other a towering sanctuary.

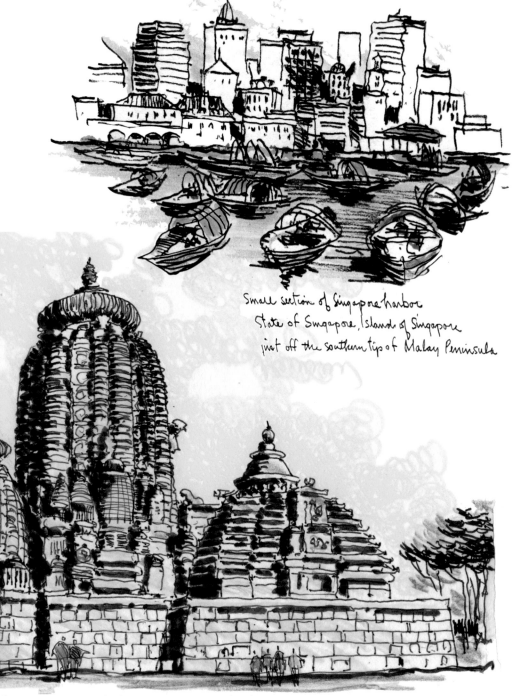

Small section of Singapore harbor
State of Singapore, Island of Singapore
just off the southern tip of Malay Peninsula

Temple of Brahmeswara at Bhubaneswar in Orissa India   two connected structures, jagamohan (assembly hall) with the Towering sanctuary sikhara

Air view of Angkor Wat

central tower
central terrace
first terrace
court yard
enclosing gallery
cruciform portal

4
3
2
5
6
1

1. Cruciform portal
2. Vishnu gallery enclosing complex
3. Courtyard
4. First terrace
5. Central terrace
6. Central tower

Angkor Wat the largest religious structure in the world

CAMBODIA

THE RUINS OF THE CAPITAL city of the old Kmer Empire are the most impressive monuments and crowning glory of Cambodian culture. ANGKOR WAT, the best-known temple, was built more than a thousand years ago by warrior-kings who were invested with divine authority. Hidden by thick jungle growth, five beautiful stone towers rise within a large rectangle of pillared galleries and buildings, all enclosed by a huge moat. Hundreds of carved figures: kings, dancers, slaves, and characters from Hindu mythology line the walls.

Main interior court within Penafiel Castle

Penafiel Castle, Spain

SPAIN

WE LOST OUR LUGGAGE on our first trip to Spain. Before we'd even left the train station, our bags somehow began a voyage in a different direction. Fortunately, we were reunited with our things upon reaching the Spanish capital.

The buildings of Madrid were impressive. And around Seville, in particular, I found castles with parapets and turrets that rivaled scenes of legendary Camelot. Under typically sunny Spanish skies, we visited one castle after another. I would eventually travel to Barcelona, to see Antonio Gaudi's structures, and other towns, but it is the south of Spain that holds the fondest memories.

La Muralla Roja Holiday Apartments

Alcazar Segovia Castilla y León — the Heartland of Spain a land of Castles

SWEDEN

Forest Crematorium, Stockholm 1940
Gunnar Asplund, Architect

Town Hall, Stockholm Sweden

1952. U.S. Embassy Stockholm Sweden

Ralph Rapson
2.0.99

64

Vacation house, Knut Knutsen

SCANDINAVIA IS WELL-KNOWN for its modern furniture, so I thought that in Sweden and Norway I would find contemporary designs in every house when I arrived in the 1950s. I was disappointed. Often the homes I visited in Stockholm and Oslo were baroque, dark, and weighted down with far too many curtains.

The architecture—new and old—didn't disappoint, however. ERIK GUNNAR ASPLUND'S FOREST CREMATORIUM and RAGNAR ÖSTBERG'S STOCKHOLM CITY HALL, arguably the city's most famous landmark, were admirable marriages of site and structure. I also had the pleasure of visiting KNUT KNUTSEN'S VACATION HOUSE—an assemblage of small staggered units that were intended to blend with nature, a pointed departure from the Modernist agenda.

Small Stave Church, near Oslo Norway

NORWAY

SWITZERLAND

I FIRST SAW SWITZERLAND from the back of a Volkswagen Beetle, which wasn't ideal. Mary and I were traveling with my partner John Van der Meulen and his wife, Norma. Since John had an affinity for these German-made cars, we rented one. We visited Lake Geneva and Lausanne. We sampled wines and basked in views of Mont Blanc.

At the time, modern buildings were few in Switzerland, but I took note of the tidiness of the citizenry and the sharp planning that had gone into the development of cities and roadways. I found intriguing the bridges of Robert Maillart, with their high arches and curving roadbeds, often located in mountain passes. Even peering from the window of the VW, the views were stunning.

Chillon Castle on Lake Geneva, Switzerland
a favorite stop over for Crusaders

Chateau Vufflen Estate
near Lake of Geneva

Simplon Pass, Switzerland.

Salginatobel Bridge
Robert Millart, Engineer

Our Lady of Lourdes, Zurich Switzerland

67

AFTER SERVING ON AN ARCHITECTURAL jury in Abu Dhabi, I continued around the world and returned home via Asia. My first stop was Bangkok, Thailand. Bangkok, with its contrasts of the very old and the very new is a bustling and fascinating city. Because of its many canals, which provide a network for commerce and travel, it is often labeled the "Amsterdam of the South." Two of my former students from MIT and Minnesota live in Bangkok. One later became a well-known architect and governor of Bangkok. He also was an avid pilot, so we flew all over the country.

THAILAND

Wat Benjamabopit
"The Marble Temple"
Bangkok

Ground travel in much of this area is indeed difficult. So as I flew over the area, I gained appreciation of both the great beauty, yet inaccessible nature of much of the landscape. The remote villages, with their unique structures, helped me gain some understanding of the people and their lives.

There were gilded temples everywhere. Most of them had orange tile roofs that turned up at the corners and edges in a style reminiscent of Chinese structures. The temple interiors were often red in color and featured gleaming structures of Buddha illuminated by a field of candles.

Though many Thai architects design strikingly modern buildings, when it came to designing a new temple, they nearly always revert to traditional forms. I remember asking an architect why he always stuck with pitched roofs when designing temples? He replied that religious and architectural traditions were so strongly interwoven that it was unthinkable that one would deviate from the classic formula. The temple form was sacred—figuratively and literally.

Rice fields in Eastern Thailand near Cambodia border

I MAY BE ONE OF THE FEW people who have seen ISTANBUL and the Straits of Bosporus from atop a minaret. I'd long wanted to see the HAGIA SOPHIA, once a mosque, a Christian church, and now a museum, and when I suggested to a guide I'd met in the streets that I'd like to see the city from one of the towers, he miraculously found a way. For twenty dollars, I not only had several meals and a day's worth of touring, but I also got to see the city's narrow, jostling streets and port from one of its finest vantage points.

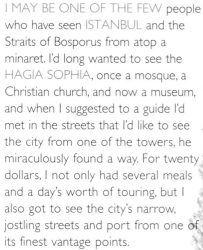

TURKEY

Hagia Sophia; Istanbul, Turkey

Skyline, Istanbul Turkey

WHILE WORKING ON PLANS for an American embassy in Beirut, a young woman and I took a government car—a black limousine with driver—into Syria and headed toward the GREAT UMAYYAD MOSQUE in Damascus. I told the driver to stop at the city limits so we could walk, but before I knew it, the car was wedging its way amid the street called "Straight"—ironically, the most winding, most narrow thoroughfare in the city. A sea of goats, merchants, and pedestrians surged around and over the car. We managed to crack open the door and escape only after considerable effort. It was one of the most embarrassing experiences of my life. How arrogant we must have seemed, Americans trying to navigate our big limo through this ancient city.

SYRIA

FROM MARBLEHEAD

Iron & steel factory
Pittsburg

Marblehead, Ma

Grain Elevators Mn

DURING MY FIRST COUPLE OF YEARS teaching at the Massachusetts Institute of Technology, I lived in nearby MARBLEHEAD, an old and picturesque fishing town on the Atlantic seaboard. Although MIT is not all that distant from Marblehead, the train commute was time-consuming and tiresome (first to Salem, then into North Station, and finally, via the subway, to Cambridge). Still, life in Marblehead, with its lazy pace, delightful vistas, and sailing activities, was more than enjoyable. At times it seemed as distant as the Pacific from my teaching work.

St Francis Mission Church, Rancho de Taos N.N. 1816

I'VE BEEN AN INLAND resident for much of my life, but Marblehead and its larger coastal cousin, San Francisco, have always retained a special place in my heart. I served for eight years on a design review committee for the City of San Francisco and never tired of visiting there. The GOLDEN GATE BRIDGE, with those great pylons and red-rust hue, never failed to charm me. It seemed the very symbol of Frisco's rich diversity, a place where cultural chasms are bridged by people daily, not without effort, but often elegantly.

TO THE GOLDEN GATE

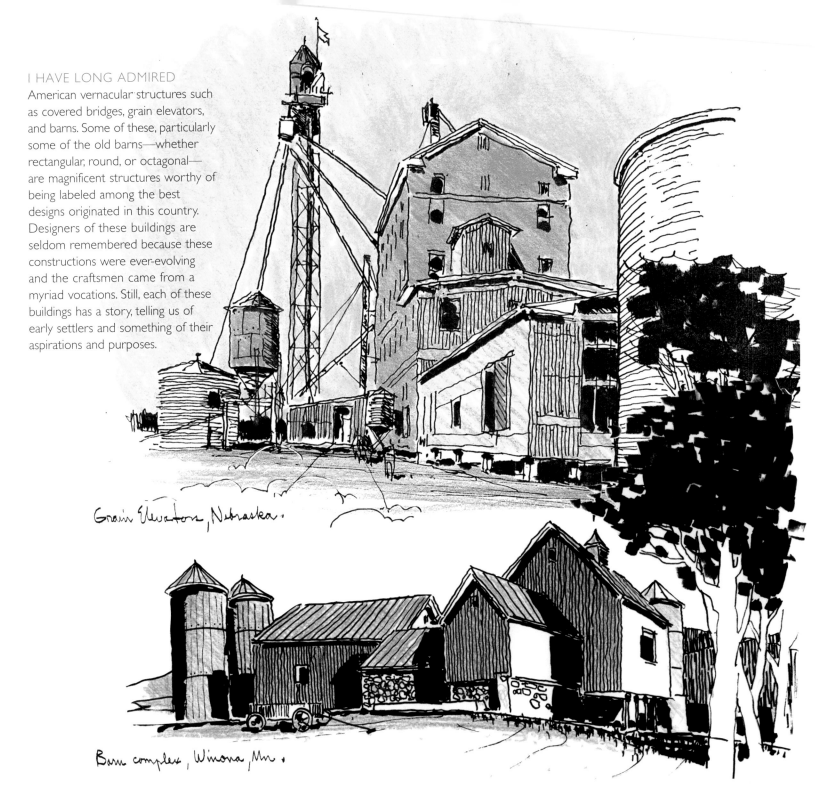

I HAVE LONG ADMIRED
American vernacular structures such
as covered bridges, grain elevators,
and barns. Some of these, particularly
some of the old barns—whether
rectangular, round, or octagonal—
are magnificent structures worthy of
being labeled among the best
designs originated in this country.
Designers of these buildings are
seldom remembered because these
constructions were ever-evolving
and the craftsmen came from a
myriad vocations. Still, each of these
buildings has a story, telling us of
early settlers and something of their
aspirations and purposes.

Grain Elevators, Nebraska.

Barn complex, Winona, Mn.

MIDWEST

Boundry Waters National Park Mn

View of Railyards Duluth Mn

Grain elevators Mpls Mn

A POPULATION CENTER in an otherwise rural area, Duluth is one of America's more interestingly sited cities. Located on the rocky granite ridge overlooking the western tip of Lake Superior, the most inland of the Great Lakes, the town commands a breathtaking vista of the bustling inland harbor. Along with its importance as a busy shipping harbor, Duluth was and continues to be an important rail and distribution center for lumber, iron ore, and agriculture. From the DULUTH RAILYARD, tracks fan out to all corners of the country.

MINNESOTA'S DE FACTO CAPITAL is large enough to support professional athletic teams, good museums, and fine music and theater organizations, yet small enough to allow contact with public officials and other VIPs. Its park system, walking paths, and bike trails further contribute to those feelings of accessibility. And through its heart flows that American icon, the Mississippi River.

Cedar Riverside
New-Town In Town
Mpls Mn. 1969
Ralph Rapson Architect

Stone Arch bridge and locks
Mississippi River, Mpls.

R. Rapson
7·94

Stone Arch Bridge
& Locks Mississippi River
Mpls Mn

R. Rapson
7 69

Teamsters Plaza Minneapolis Mn

In a sense, Minneapolis is a traditional city of small homes, so the style of living has generally been one family per residence. My work at CEDAR RIVERSIDE, a complex of integrated living environments located a short distance from the Mississippi, brought a different feeling to the city. Its various pieces, from a forty-floor tower to smaller one- and two-story structures, anticipated more modern urban living at higher densities.

PROSPECT PARK

DIRECTLY ACROSS THE STREET from our home on Seymour Avenue in Minneapolis is a small park—approximately one block square. Its name, Prospect Park, has become the moniker for the entire area. An old water tower crowns the hill in the park, the highest elevation in the city. Its conical, tiled roof has earned it the name "WITCHES' TOWER."

Some years ago, a strong storm ripped off some of the roof tiles. City officials decided to tear down the upper part of the tower, but the community rose up in outcry: scouts sold cookies, and citizens protested and paraded until the city finally reversed its wrong-headed decision. The beauty of the tower was preserved, and it was far cheaper than demolition.

I have drawn and painted the tower hundreds of times. I suspect there is hardly a home in Prospect Park that does not boast one of these drawings.

Witch's Tower
Prospect Park Mn.

THE ARCHITECTURE OF MINNESOTA ranges from classical to contemporary. Two of the finest structures are the STATE CAPITOL in St. Paul and the CHURCH AT SAINT JOHN'S UNIVERSITY in Collegeville. The capitol building, designed by Cass Gilbert, is among the most handsome state capitols in the country. Marcel Breuer's church at Saint John's is equally striking in its own right: The sculptural bell that fronts the building can be seen from quite a distance, serving as a climactic centerpiece for the small-town college campus.

MINNESOTA

St. John's Abbey and University Church, Collegeville, Mn   1970

Minnesota State Capitol   St Paul Mn   1904   Cass Gilbert   Architect

81

NEW YORK CITY

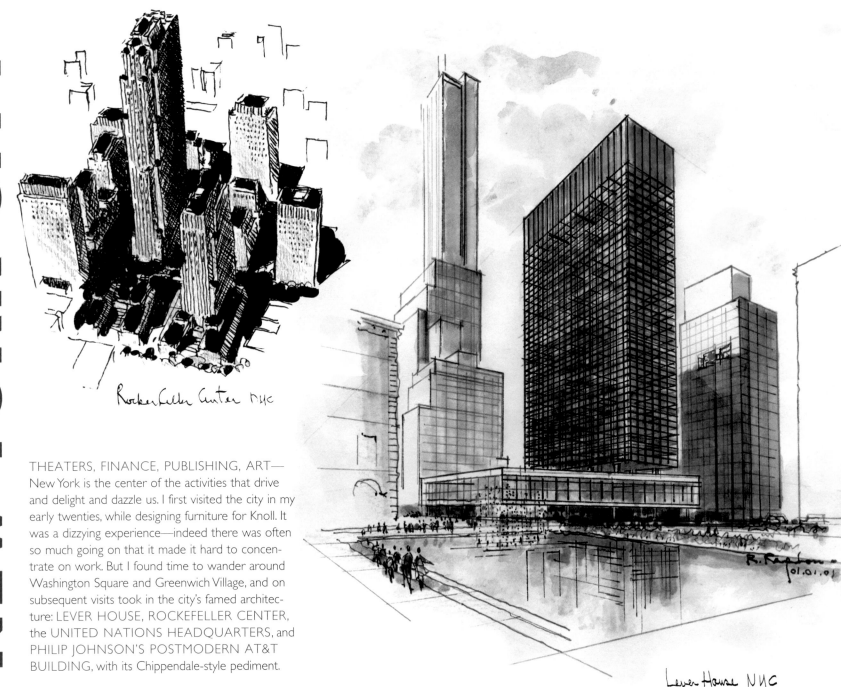

Rockefeller Center NYC

THEATERS, FINANCE, PUBLISHING, ART—
New York is the center of the activities that drive
and delight and dazzle us. I first visited the city in my
early twenties, while designing furniture for Knoll. It
was a dizzying experience—indeed there was often
so much going on that it made it hard to concentrate on work. But I found time to wander around
Washington Square and Greenwich Village, and on
subsequent visits took in the city's famed architecture: LEVER HOUSE, ROCKEFELLER CENTER,
the UNITED NATIONS HEADQUARTERS, and
PHILIP JOHNSON'S POSTMODERN AT&T
BUILDING, with its Chippendale-style pediment.

Lever House NYC

American Telegraph & Telephone Company

Philip Johnson Architect

New York City

United Nations Headquarters

83

SAN FRANCISCO

San Francisco skyline 1943 — R. Rapsing '93

SAN FRANCISCO—A FAVORITE of almost everyone—is one of the world's most fascinating and beautiful cities. When I first visited there, towers stood on the tops of hills and inland, while shorter buildings hugged the coast. Sadly, skyscrapers in the city's financial district have since eclipsed such a view—one of the most striking urban panoramas I've ever observed.

Built on many hills, the city takes on an aura in late afternoon that has led residents of Chinatown to call the place "Gum San," or "Golden Hill." I happened once to witness the CHINESE NEW YEAR in San Francisco, a celebration that brings dragons into the streets. Each monster has its own particular colors, shapes, and designs, and is accompanied by dancers in costume, equally colorful.

Chinese New Year, San Francisco

THE TALLEST OF MY CONSTRUCTED BUILDINGS reached just forty floors—Minneapolis's Cedar-Riverside Towers. From SIR NORMAN FOSTER'S COMMERZBANK headquarters in Frankfurt, replete with nine garden spaces spiraling up the structure, to CESAR PELLI'S STUNNING TWIN TOWERS in Malaysia—the world's highest designs continue to evolve. Glass curtains and steel frames have become the modern language of the metropolis.

HIGH TOWERS

Commerzbank Headquarters, Frankfurt Germany Foster + Partners

John Hancock Building, Chicago, Ill. 1970 Bruce Graham of S.O.M. Architects

Petronas Towers, Kuala Lumpur Malaysia Cesàr Pelli Architect

Post Office Tower, London

Bank of China Hong Kong China, England—
I. M. Pei Architect

Hong Kong-Shanghi Bank, Hong Kong China   Norman Foster Architect

87

I HAVE BEEN FORTUNATE to have known and worked with many of the giants of modern architecture—architects, planners, designers, and writers who have shaped the basic principals of our built environment.

Among those titans are people like Sven Markelius, of Sweden; Eliel Saarinen and Alvar Aalto, of Finland; Auguste Perret and Le Corbusier, of France; Walter Gropius and Marcel Breuer, of Germany and the Bauhaus; Mies van der Rohe and Laszlo Maholy-Nagy, also of the Bauhaus; Siegfried Giedeon, chronicler of CIAM and author of *Space, Time and Architecture*; historian Henry-Russell Hitchcock; Richard Neutra, of Los Angeles; George Fred Keck, of Chicago; Serge Chermayeff and Eric Mendelsohn; Felix Candela, of Mexico; Buckminster Fuller; and, of course, Frank Lloyd Wright.

I also knew many of those who followed in their wake: Eero Saarinen, Paolo Soleri, José Luis Sert, Louis Kahn, Harwell Hamilton Harris, William Wilson Wurster; Peter Blake, Philip Johnson, Gordon Bunshaft, John Johansen, Walter Netch, Eduardo Catalano, Hans Knoll, Minoru Yamasaki, Harry Weese, John Entenza and Charles Eames—all of them, great talents and interesting individuals.

It is quite impossible to include drawings of work by each one of these designers, but a few are presented here.

Musée d'Orsay, Paris controversial interior treatment by Gae Aulenti in 1986
Original Beaux-Arts Railway Station by Victor Laloux 1898

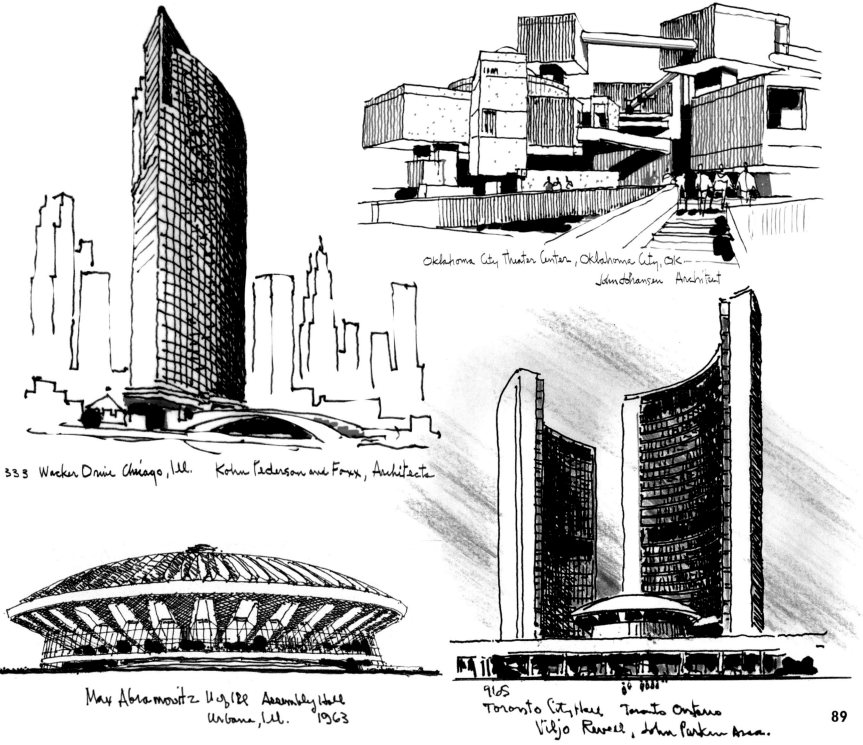

Oklahoma City Theater Center, Oklahoma City, OK.
John Johansen, Architect

333 Wacker Drive Chicago, Ill.   Kohn Pederson and Foxx, Architects

Max Abramovitz Uof Ill Assembly Hall
Urbana, Ill.   1963

9165
Toronto City Hall Toronto Ontario
Viljo Revell, John Parkin Asso.

89

Lowell Health house
Los Angles, Ca.
Richard Neutra

Einstein Tower, 1921
Dome observatory
& astrophysical lab.

Erich Mendelsohn, Arch.

Arcosanti near Cordes Junction Arizona
1970
Paolo Soleri

Farnsworth House   Mies van der Rohe Architect

90

Apartment building Berlin Germany
Walter Gropius Architect

Exeter Library Exeter, New Hampshire

Sea Ranch Condominium, Sea Ranch, CA. Moore Lyndon Turnbull Whitaker
Architects

Cadet Chapel, Air Force Academy, Colorado Springs Colorado
Walter Netsch, S.OM Architects

91

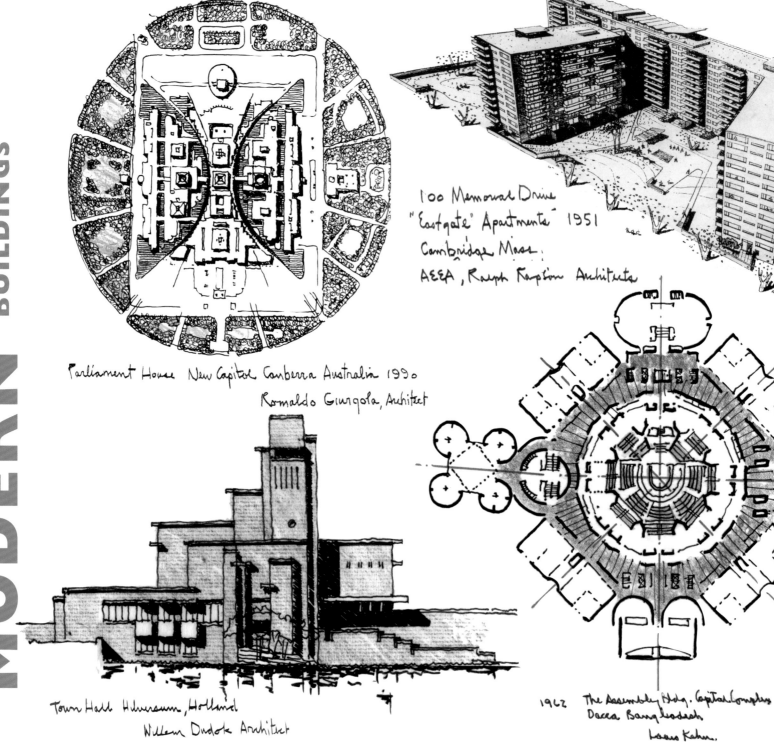

Parliament House New Capitol Canberra Australia 1990
Romaldo Giurgola, Architect

100 Memorial Drive
"Eastgate" Apartments 1951
Cambridge Mass.
AEEA, Ralph Rapson Architects

Town Hall Hilversum, Holland
Willem Dudok Architect

1962 The Assembly Bldg. Capitol Complex
Dacca Bangladesh
Louis Kahn.

92

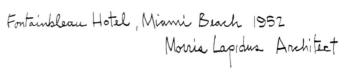

Fontainbleau Hotel, Miami Beach 1952
Morris Lapidus Architect

Ralph Rapson entry for
the "Jefferson Arch Competition"

Jefferson Memorial Arch St Louis, Mo
Eero Saarinen, Architect

RELIGIOUS

Open Chapel of Lomas Mexico 1959
Felix Candela, Architect

Bahá-i House of Worship, New Delhi, India

I HAVE DONE MANY DRAWINGS of cathedrals and churches, but some of the most interesting religious buildings I've encountered have been dedicated to faiths foreign to me or to purposes other than worship. The lotus-like curves of a modern BAHÁ'I TEMPLE in India, for example, are an engineering marvel, reminiscent of the concrete-dome constructions of Spanish architect Felix Candela in Mexico. The dome of the NAMUGONGO SHRINE in Uganda is a steel memorial laden with traditional carvings depicting the murder of several Christian converts in the 1800s.

St Oswald Church and Rectory
Austria

Church of the Annunciation, Greek Orthodox 1956
Frank Lloyd Wright Architect

Namugongo Martyrs Shrine, Uganda

95

THE OPPORTUNITY TO EXPERIENCE firsthand some of the early work of Le Corbusier was indeed memorable. Le Corbusier was and remains one of the greatest modern architects, and he was one of my early idols.

Corbu was not an easy man to get to know. I think he was really quite contemptuous of most designers. We met a few times while I was living in France in the 1950s. Once, I attended a gala evening as part of the CIAM (Congrès Internationaux d'Architecture Moderne) conference held at his Unité d'Habitation near Marseilles. The rooftop garden was a throng of music, conversation, and lively dancing while stars and city lights twinkled magically. The architect was surprisingly complimentary about the design I was doing for U.S. staff housing—though it was a scheme much influenced by Corbu's own work.

Notre-Dame du Haut 1954 Le Corbusier Architect
pilgrim chapel near Ronchamp, France.

Villa at Garches, France

Le Corbusier / La Tourette Eveux
France

Le Corbusier Architect

Le Rapieon
(after Le Corbusier)

My unfinished sketch of one of Corbus drawings

SAARINENS

Eliel Saarinen: Helsinki Railroad Station

Christ Lutheran Church Minneapolis, Mn. 1948 Eliel Saarinen Architect

IT WAS MY GREAT good fortune to have had the experience of studying and working with Eliel Saarinen and his son Eero Saarinen. Over the years we maintained our friendship and professional association.

Eliel and Eero Saarinen remain perhaps the most distinguished father and son architects the world has seen. The dapper, stylish father, Eliel, was the foremost Finnish architect to forge new and powerful architectural forms, overthrowing the Beaux Arts tradition. Later, his elegant entry in the Chicago Tribune Competition brought him world-wide recognition and spurred his immigration to this country to become an architect and planner for the world-famous Cranbrook Academy of Art.

Silver Urn and Tray 1934

Crow Island School, Winnetka, Ill. Eliel Saarinen Architect

Eero Saarinen Terminal Building, Dulles International Airport Chantilly, Va. 1963

EERO SAARINEN followed in his father's tradition to become a leading architect of the modern era. Like his father, who designed the Helsinki railway station, Eero made his most memorable marks in transportation, with the Dulles International Airport building in Chantilly, Virginia, and the TWA terminal at New York's Idlewild (now John F. Kennedy) Airport. The son was considerably more casual than his father, however, and while Eliel devised only a few studies for a project, Eero churned out dozens before he was satisfied with a design.

Eero and I worked together on a number of projects, one being the competition for a festival theater and fine arts center for William and Mary College in 1928. Our entry received First Award!

Pedestal Chair studies 1955

Administration Center, John Deere Company, Moline, Il.
1961
Eero Saarinen

General Motors Technical Center, Warren, Mich. 1956 Eero Saarinen

WHILE A STUDENT at Michigan, I traveled to Taliesin with two of my peers to meet the great Frank Lloyd Wright. The architect had started a fellowship program at Taliesin, where students worked and studied in the shadow of the master. While I admired Wright's designs, his Spring Green, Wisconsin, retreat seemed to me too somber and monastic. There wasn't the laughter, joy, and chaos that I was used to. Wright, meantime, seemed to realize that we didn't have sufficient money to attend Taliesin and made my friends and I the butt of a screed on the perils of architectural education.

Robie house, Chicago, Ill, 1909

Taliesin East Spring Green, Wisconsin

Price Tower (office and apartment building) Bartlesville, Ok 1956
Frank Lloyd Wright Architect

Years later, whenever I encountered him at Cranbrook or the University of Minnesota, he would look me up and down and say, "So this is where you ended up." While I appreciate his work greatly, and have since encountered a house he built in Okemos, Michigan, near my hometown of Alma, I have never attempted—nor should others—to use his personal architectural vocabulary.

Falling Water (Kaufman House) Bear Run, Penn. 1935
Frank Lloyd Wright Architect.

Taliesin West

Prince of Peace Lutheran Church
for the Deaf   St. Paul, Mn.

Chapel-in-the-Hills North Dakota 1972

Hope Lutheran
Church Mpls
1970   Rapson Ave.

St Peters Lutheran Church, Edina Mn. 1957

DESIGNING A RELIGIOUS BUILDING is always a challenge. Next to one's home, nothing triggers an emotional response like the design of a church or synagogue. One of the most satisfying churches I worked on was the PRINCE OF PEACE LUTHERAN CHURCH FOR THE DEAF in St. Paul. The congregation loved the building, and whenever I visited they would embrace me or clap me on the back to show their happiness. I seldom have done a project where people have been so sincerely appreciative of the work.

The forms and spaces of ST. PETER'S CHURCH, with its altar surrounded by the congregation stemmed from the concept of the "family of God" gathered around the Lord's table. In a sense, it anticipated my later Guthrie design.

Adath-Beth El Chapel. Crystal Mn
Rapson Fishman Architects

103

Arts and Science Center St. Paul Mn 1959

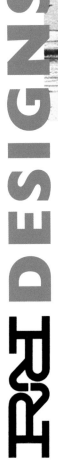

RRT DESIGNS

SIGNIFICANT DESIGN CAN only be achieved by totality of the creative act and totality of the entire design and development process. This involves historical continuity, sensitive responses to site and ecological conditions, an understanding of both the physical and psychological needs of society, and a full knowledge of structural, material, and technological considerations.

If architecture is to achieve the quality of true art through creative space, form, and place, however, design must go beyond the reality of the items mentioned above and speak to their more subjective and meaningful aspects. We must respond to the great potentials of our time.

Performing Arts, Fine Arts & Music Center, 1971
University of California
Santa Cruz, CA

Adath Beth El Chapel
Crystal Mn
Rapson Fishman Architects

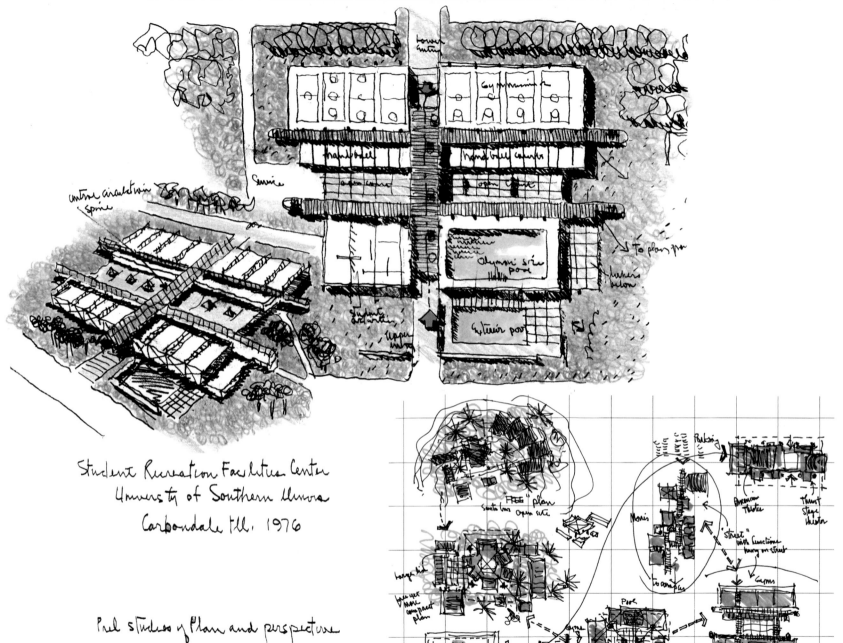

Student Recreation Facilities Center
University of Southern Illinois
Carbondale Ill. 1976

Prel studies of Plan and perspective

Planning diagram - relationships of
several institutional type projects

105

DURING MY STUDENT days and early career, participating in a design competition was often one of the best ways to win a choice commission or professional recognition. I entered several—both as collaborator and sole designer—and often won. The schemes varied: A traveling competition such as the Booth, a theater arts center at William and Mary College, planning and housing for Chicago and Roosevelt Island, a number of small house competitions, as well as designs for furniture and lighting.

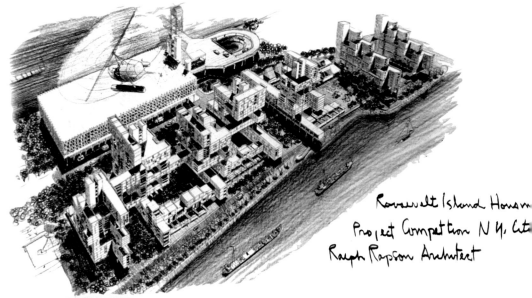

Roosevelt Island Housing
Project Competition N.Y. City
Ralph Rapson Architect

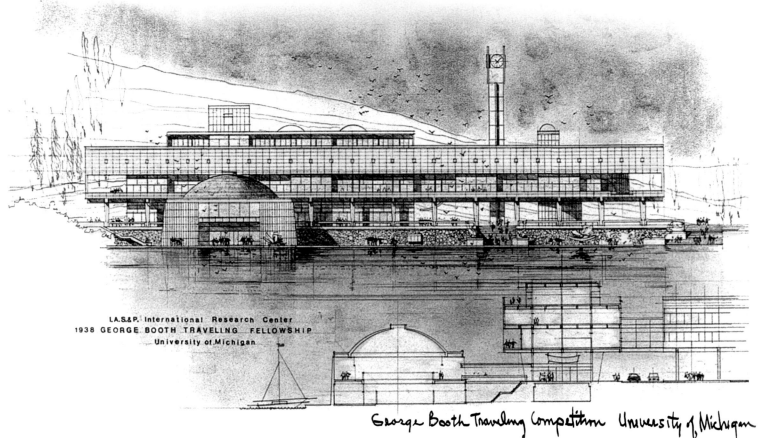

I.A.S.&P. International Research Center
1938 GEORGE BOOTH TRAVELING FELLOWSHIP
University of Michigan

George Booth Traveling Competition University of Michigan

Lentz-Polesky House Golden Valley, Mn.
Toby & Ralph Rapson Architects

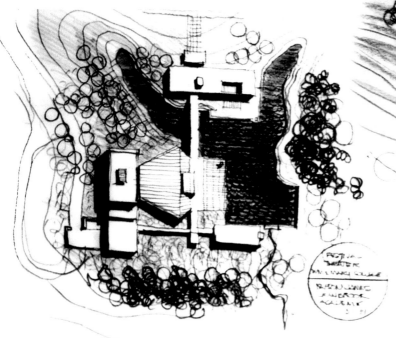

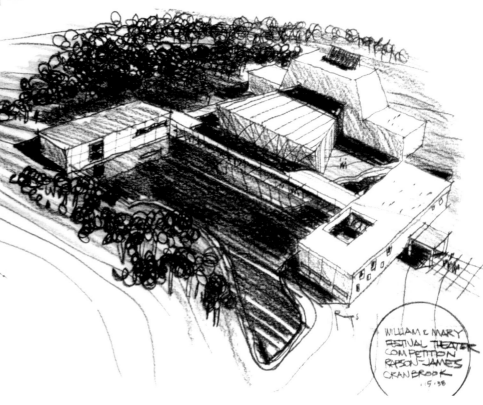

Festival Theater and Fine Arts Center, William and Mary College, 1938

FOLLOWING WORLD WAR II, the United States stepped up its role on the international stage and, in conjunction with the Marshall Plan, began building embassies throughout the world. Through my friendship with H.G. Knoll, I was invited to Washington to speak to members of the Foreign Buildings Operation of the State Department.

I was an instructor at MIT at the time, and had resisted taking commissions in order to concentrate full-time on teaching. But I soon discovered that students were eager to see their teachers not only as professors, but as practitioners. When the State Department offered me several embassy commissions, I immediately requested what I assumed would be a short leave of absence and booked passage on a ship to Holland with my wife, Mary, and my partner, John Van der Meulen, and his wife.

The Hague, Stockholm, Copenhagen, Oslo, Bremen, and Athens—I worked with American officials and local architects in each of these cities to realize this new international presence in the form of embassies and consulates. The results were always modern, but sensitive to the sites and architectural traditions of the cities that surrounded them.

U.S. Embassy Stockholm, Sweden 1951
preliminary study

U.S. Embassy Athens Greece 1953

U.S. Embassy Den Hague Netherlands 1951

U.S. Embassy Copenhagen
Denmark 1952

109

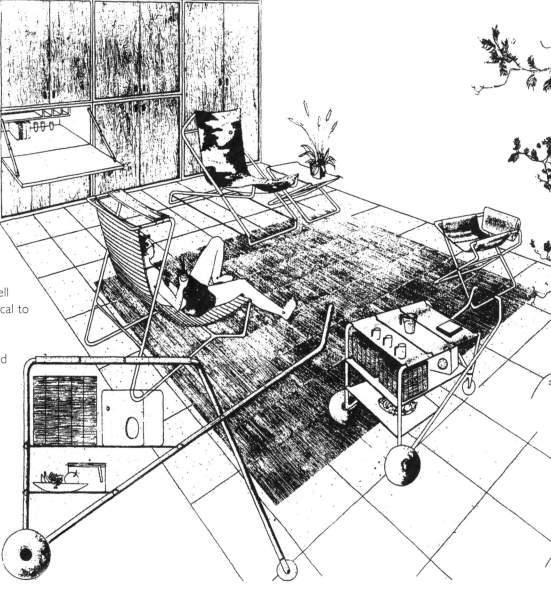

EQUIPMENT

MY INTEREST IN THE DESIGN of what I call "equipment for living" dates from my studies at the Cranbrook Academy of Art in Bloomfield Hills, Michigan. Working my way through an integrated curriculum that pushed me to try my hand at almost every type of artistic discipline, I met such talented and dedicated people as Harry Bertoia, Charles Eames, and Eero Saarinen. It was a most compelling experience.

Designing products for living is exciting and rewarding. The designer must marry technology considerations with the realities of product use and the whims of the human psyche. All the senses—sight, touch, sound, and smell—are attuned to function and, thereby, pleasure.

In a sense, my approach to furniture and furnishings design is much the same as my approach to architecture. The human body serves as the yardstick, and while contemporary living has evolved considerably over the decades, the measure remains the same. Experience, as well as function, materials, and aesthetics, remains critical to the design.

Many of my designs for tableware, ceramics, lighting, and furniture were done between 1938 and 1940, during my Cranbrook years. Others were done for H. G. Knoll Associates, a New York City-based furniture company.

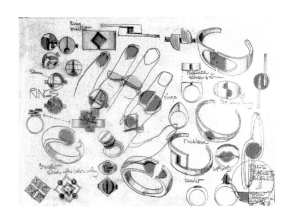

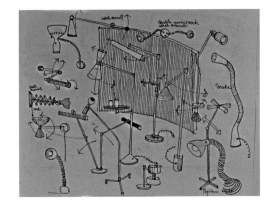

Rapson "Chair-of-Tomorrow" 1942

111

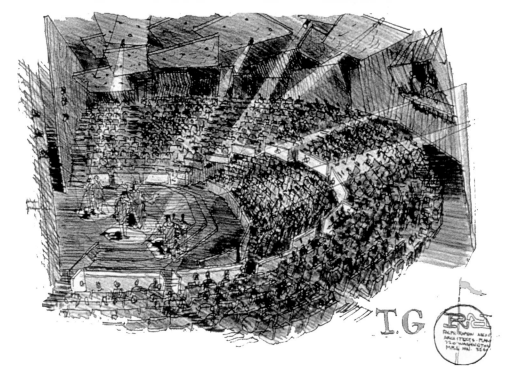

THE DESIGN FOR THE GUTHRIE

Theater represented one of the most challenging assignments available. Sir Tyrone Guthrie ("Sir Tyrant"), the pre-eminent director of theater at the time, and his colleagues decided to set up a regional repertory theater company in Minneapolis.

Working with the legendary director proved both exciting and frustrating; our notions about theater design and the architect's role were markedly different. My design incorporated an asymmetrical seating arrangement around a thrust stage and modern interior and exterior architectural expressions—elements that rankled some conservative tastes.

GUTHRIE

Rapson "Glass Cube"
Little Falls Wis.
1973

Ralph Rapson
1.27.99

IN 1972 MY WIFE AND I purchased forty acres near Amery, Wisconsin, on which to build a vacation house. Every time I suggested a scheme, however, Mary complained that the views of the meadows, the bluffs, the pines or the Apple River would be blocked. The result was an all-glass cube. By day the views—and the sunrises and sunsets—are magnificent. At night, the house becomes a luminescent jewel.

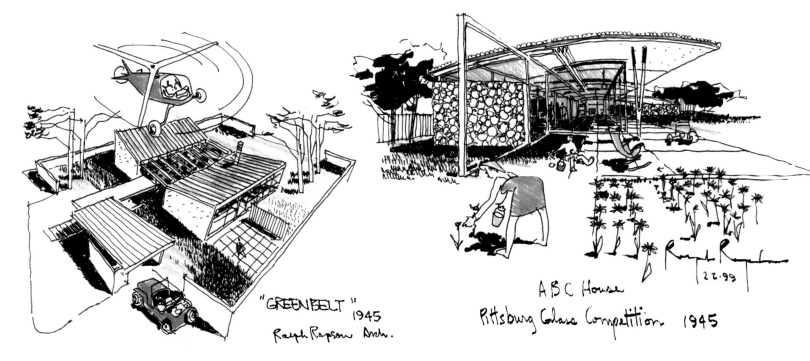

"GREENBELT" 1945
Ralph Rapson Arch.

ABC House
Pittsburg Glass Competition 1945

I HAVE DESIGNED MANY HOUSES; a few were large residences, but most were small and inexpensive homes. I find designing small-budget homes that any person might live in a more challenging and satisfying experience than laying plans for larger homes.

Hagberg House and Studio, Mount Pleasant Michigan 1940
Ralph Rapson Architect

Jack Graff summer house Grand Rapids Mn. 2001

Pillsbury Residence Wayzata Mn 1963

Gidwitz House, Chicago Illinois 1946

These houses have been careful responses to the sites, needs, and aspirations of my clients. More "international style" in flavor than the "naturalistic" homes of Frank Lloyd Wright and others, my designs are finished in white and complemented by bold colors.

I'm also pleased to note that many of my residential clients have remained my life-long friends—a gratifying achievement.

Gourley Residence University Grove 1966
Falcon Heights Mn.

Kern Residence, Lincoln Mass 1954

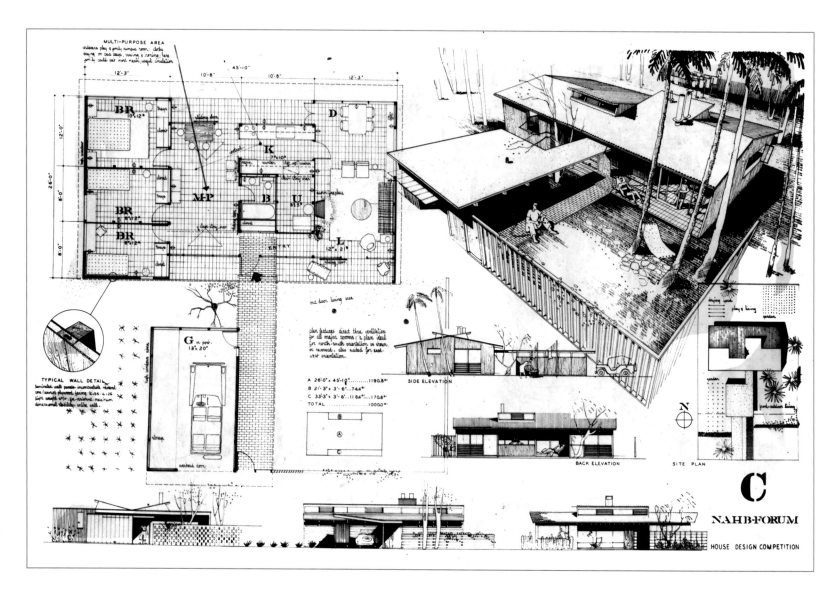

Within the drawing, the following labels are visible:

MULTI-PURPOSE AREA
children's play & family rumpus room : cloths drying on sun days, ironing & mending here gym & could use north wash wept circulation

MULTI-PURPOSE AREA

BR
10'×12'

BR
8'×12'

BR
8'×12'

M-P

K
7'×10'

B

U

D

L
12'×21'

ENTRY

G or port.
13'×20'

TYPICAL WALL DETAIL
laminated wall panels incombustible material

out door living area

plan features direct thru ventilation for all major rooms : a plan ideal for north-south orientation as shown, or reversed, also suited for east-west orientation.

A 26'·0" × 45'·10"..........1190.8"
B 21'·3" × 3'· 6"......74.4"
C 33'·3" × 3'· 6"...1164"....170.8"
TOTAL ....1000.0"

SIDE ELEVATION

BACK ELEVATION

SITE PLAN

N

C

NAHB-FORUM

HOUSE DESIGN COMPETITION

IN 1950, THE NATIONAL ASSOCIATION of Home Builders held a nationwide housing competition for a small 1,000-square-foot house plan tailored to a particular region of the country. Amazingly, the com- petition drew some seven thousand entries, making it the largest com- petition in its day. The rules permitted only one entry per person, but since I had worked out two designs, I decided to enter one in Mary's

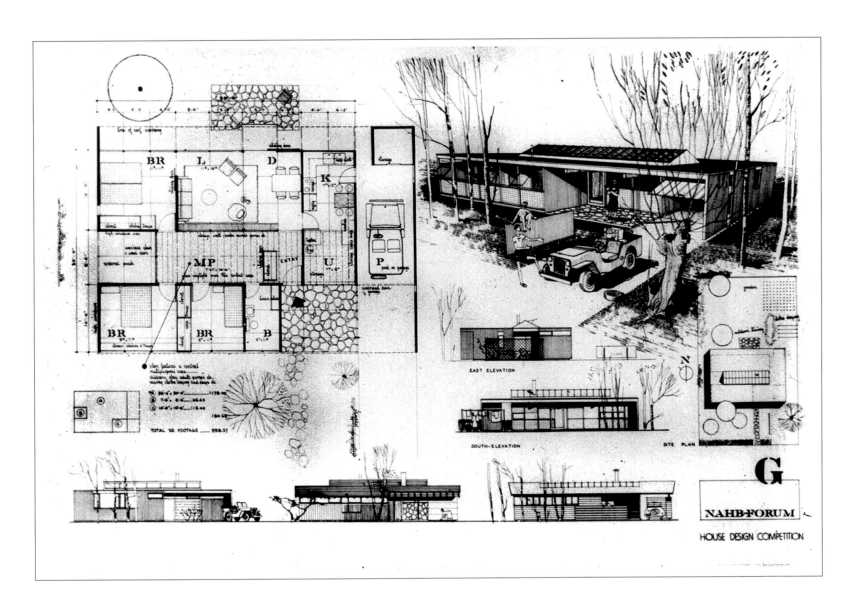

Labels visible within the drawing:

BR L D K MP ENTRY U P BR BR B

TOTAL SQ FOOTAGE 998.37

EAST ELEVATION

SOUTH ELEVATION

SITE PLAN

N

G

NAHB·FORUM

HOUSE DESIGN COMPETITION

name. At the last moment, I flipped a coin to decide how to credit the designs. The entry submitted under my name received second national overall prize and first prize for homes designed for the southeast region.

The other entry won nothing. What would have happened if the coin flip had resulted in Mary's name on the winning award? My winning entry is the one on the page opposite.

LIFE DRAWINGS

I'VE OFTEN SAID IF YOU CAN draw the human figure, you can draw anything. It's one of the hardest things to render.

You can certainly be a great architect without being able to draw, but drawing helps one analyze and feel an object or a scene. Every time I put down a line—thick or thin, smooth or shaky—it begins to say something to me about the space or figure that's being drawn. While computers are essential to modern architectural practice and capable of astonishing feats, no program has yet been written that can render a face or figure with the sensitivity and nuance that drawing by hand communicates.

These drawings of a female nude were done on red, blue, and orange construction paper while I was at Cranbrook. I often found myself using whatever materials were available.